*We Sing from the Heart: How The Slants® Took Their Fight for
Free Speech to the Supreme Court*
Text copyright © 2024 Mia Wenjen
Illustrations copyright © 2024 Victor Bizar Gómez

Song lyrics reproduced by permission of The Slants LLC

Published in 2024 by Red Comet Press, LLC, Brooklyn, NY

Distributed in North America by ABRAMS, New York

Library of Congress Control Number: 2023941955

ISBN (HB): 978-1-63655-087-9
ISBN (EBOOK): 978-1-63655-088-6

24 25 26 27 TLF 10 9 8 7 6 5 4 3 2 1

First Edition
Manufactured in China

REDCOMETPRESS.COM

MIA WENJEN   VICTOR BIZAR GÓMEZ

WE SING
FROM THE
HEART

HOW THE SLANTS® TOOK THEIR FIGHT FOR
FREE SPEECH TO THE SUPREME COURT

RED COMET PRESS · BROOKLYN

STORIES MATTER.

Growing up, I heard this often, but I didn't really understand what it meant until my own story was on the line. You don't want others defining who you are or telling your story because you are complex, talented, and more special than any one simple definition.

Your uniqueness is your greatest strength. That's your song, and that's the one you want others to sing. And you never know how that song will change the world.

So it's true: stories do matter, but who tells them matters, too. Tell your story, sing your songs, and don't be afraid to make some trouble.

Simon Tam

AN ICY WIND blasted Simon's face as he walked out of the chamber into the late morning sun. For the first time his shoulders relaxed.

He wanted to make sure that no one could copy his band's name, The Slants. This was the last stop of a battle that started nearly eight years ago.

Simon was used to being on stage in front of an enthusiastic audience, but this time was different. This crowd wasn't here to dance. They were hoping to see history being made, but it would take months before they would get their answer.

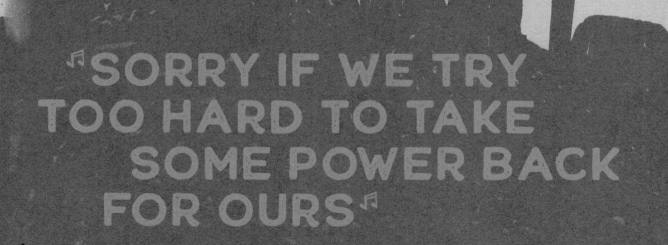

♬"SORRY IF WE TRY TOO HARD TO TAKE SOME POWER BACK FOR OURS"♬

"NO, WE WON'T BE COMPLACENT KNOW IT'S A ROCK N ROLL NATION

SIMON WAS DRAWN to music as a toddler, staging "concerts" on his dad's guitar even though he didn't know how to play. In elementary school, he discovered pop music through his father's record collection and decided to learn bass guitar. It was the perfect instrument for a future punk rocker.

"Our kid really wants to be a rock star!"

"Let's hope he grows out of that when he gets older."

But Simon kept strumming and turned the stereo up louder. He looked at the television and thought, "I'm going to play music on TV one day."

♪ THERE'S NO ROOM FOR YOUR BACKWARD FEELINGS AND YOUR BACKYARD DEALINGS ♪

WHEN SIMON WAS in middle school, four older boys approached him. One threw sand in his face. As Simon wiped his eyes, another kicked him in the stomach.

"Look at this Jap! I can't believe sand can even fit in those slits."

"This gook isn't going to do anything."

Their lips curled as they laughed.

"I'm a Chink! Get it right! You guys are so stupid, you can't even be racist right."

Simon's words stopped his attackers. For the first time, he realized that taking ownership of a stereotype gave him power.

Jap: a racist slur against someone of Japanese descent

Gook: a racist slur against Asians, particularly those of Filipino, Korean, or Vietnamese descent

Chink: a racist slur against someone of Chinese descent

♫**THE LANGUAGE OF OPPRESSION WILL LOSE TO EDUCATION UNTIL THE WORDS CAN'T HURT US AGAIN**♫

AT HIS FAMILY'S restaurant in San Diego, California, Simon's cheeks flushed when he overheard his mother taking food orders.

"I want some flied lice!"

"Chicken flied liiiice and Egg Frow-wah soup."

When the world made Simon feel small, music was a safe place.

SIMON'S PASSION WAS music, but it wasn't a career his parents approved of. He was nearly done with college, but he felt like he was going down the wrong path. In need of a fresh start, he decided to give up his college scholarship, move away from family, and join a rock band.

"Son, if moving will make you happy, you should go."

"We just want you to smile again."

He was ready to chase his dream of being a musician.

♪ "SO SORRY IF YOU TAKE OFFENSE BUT SILENCE WILL NOT MAKE AMENDS"♪

WHEN SIMON LOOKED around, he didn't see many people who looked like him—Asians weren't on television or in bands. Something needed to change. He decided to start an all-Asian American band, but what to call it?

He asked his friends, "What is something that all Asians have in common?"

They rolled their eyes and said, "Slanted eyes."

He named his new band The Slants as a way to take ownership of hurtful words and give them a new meaning.

♫"SORRY IF OUR VOICE IS TOO RAW♫"

SIMON DISCOVERED THAT there was another band, made up of non-Asians, with the same name. A friend asked, "Have you ever thought about applying to register your trademark? That might help with any confusion."

He tried to register the band's name with the government so only their band would be able to use it. It should have been easy. But it wasn't.

Trademark: Something that identifies the source of goods or services in the form of a word, a phrase, or a logo. Trademark law protects a brand's name by discouraging other businesses from using something similar that would cause confusion.

Famous trademarks for bands include The Rolling Stones' hot lips logo, The Monkees logo shaped like a guitar, and AC/DC's lightning bolt.

♫ SORRY IF YOU TAKE OFFENSE YOU MAKE UP RULES AND PLAY PRETEND ♫

A FEW MONTHS LATER, Simon heard back. His trademark for The Slants was rejected because the U.S. Patent and Trademark office determined the band's name to be racist. How could his Asian American band be racist against Asians?

At first Simon thought this was a practical joke. Then he was angry because the government's ruling was based on a photo of a pop star and her friends pulling their eyelids back in a racist pose. Any middle school teacher would have rejected this "evidence."

"Who did the Trademark Office say was actually offended by our name?"

"No one."

U.S. Patent and Trademark Office® :
A government office that issues patents and trademark registration for products and intellectual property identification to individuals and businesses.

WHY WERE ASIANS being treated differently by the government? It wasn't fair.

"I can't afford to keep fighting this thing."

"Simon, I understand, but you have to know that this case is a lot bigger than your band."

Simon realized that if he could show that the judicial system was racist, he could right a history of wrongs. He decided to fight for his rights—in court.

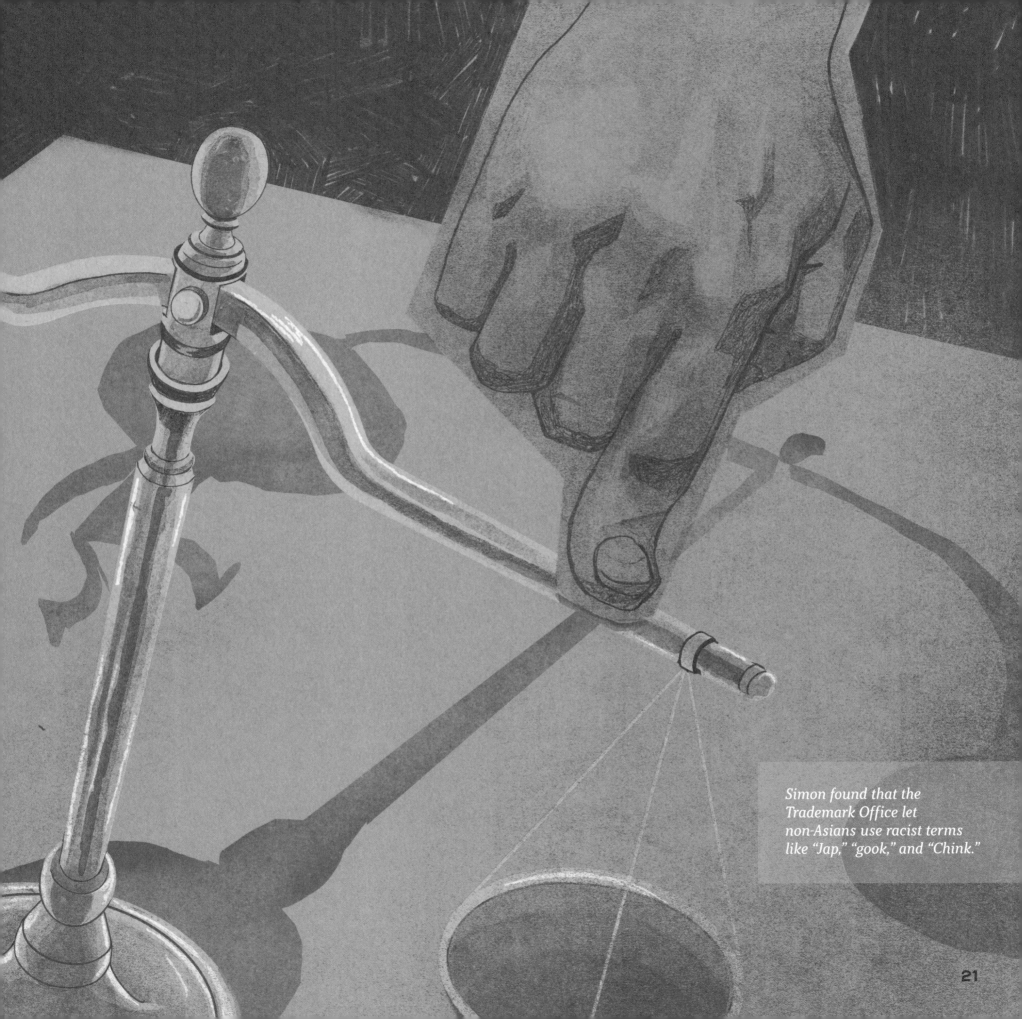

Simon found that the Trademark Office let non-Asians use racist terms like "Jap," "gook," and "Chink."

♪ **THE SYSTEM'S ALL WRONG AND IT WON'T BE LONG BEFORE THE KIDS ARE SINGING OUR SONG** ♪

FIRED UP, SIMON talked to Asian American leaders in his community and online. Everyone wanted him to keep fighting, so he went to court to make his case.

"If we don't win, we're going to appeal. We're going to use every option for you, even if this has to go to the Supreme Court."

Two thousand pages of support came pouring in but was not enough. Simon lost his case, but he refused to give up, and The Slants continued to perform.

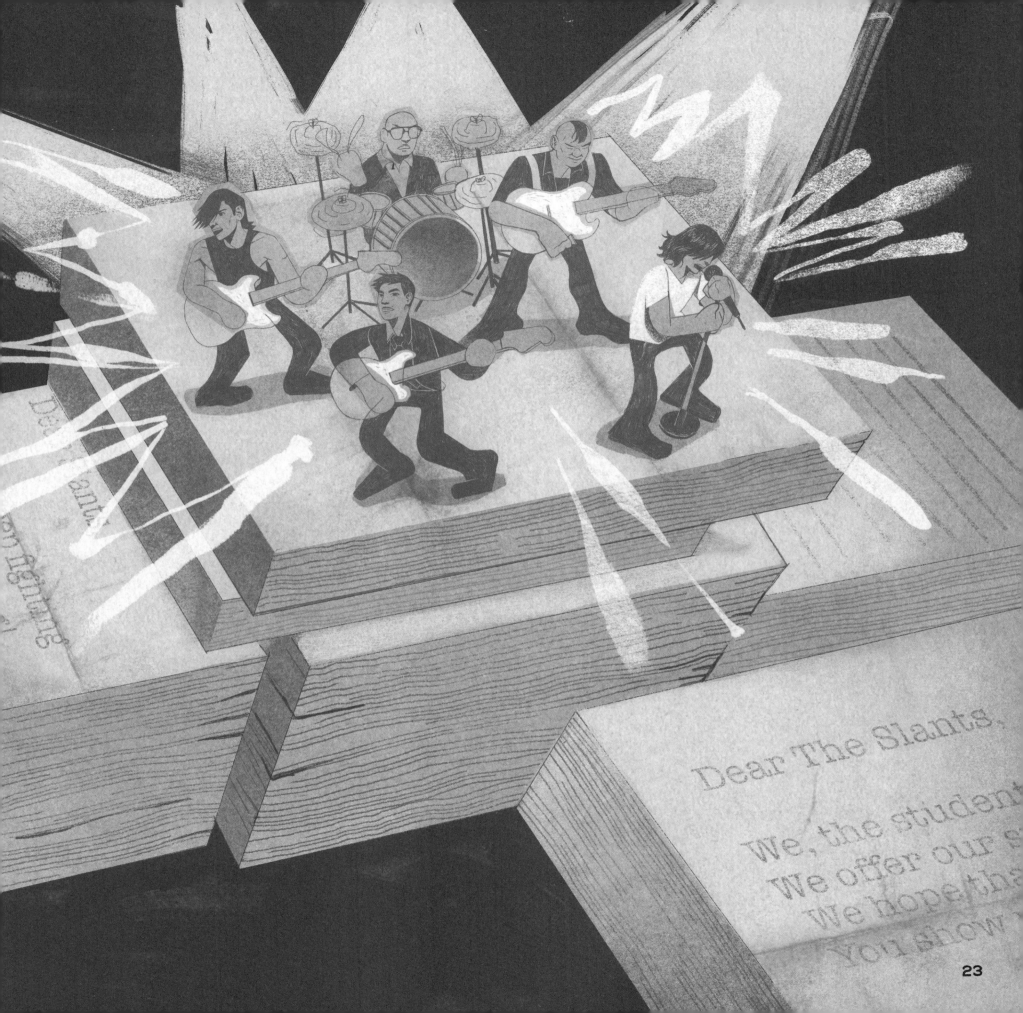

♪ **SORRY IF OUR NOTES ARE TOO SHARP** ♪

AS THE SLANTS drew larger and larger crowds, Simon became a role model for Asian American kids. Young fans wrote letters to thank him for giving them a band they could be proud of. Others found hope in how Simon fought for his right to words, any words, as he wanted.

"Ever since elementary school, we learned about the band who was willing to fight for our community."

"Thank you for showing us that we can have power."

THE SLANTS CASE would now be decided by the Supreme Court, the highest court in the United States!

The night before his case, Simon was exhausted. He had spent the week giving interview after interview, capped by a live concert featuring their new song about their trademark battle.

As Simon finished dinner at a Chinese restaurant, he carefully cracked open his fortune cookie. It was a good omen.

♫"NO, WE WON'T REMAIN SILENT"♫

A JUDGMENT WILL SOON RULE IN YOUR

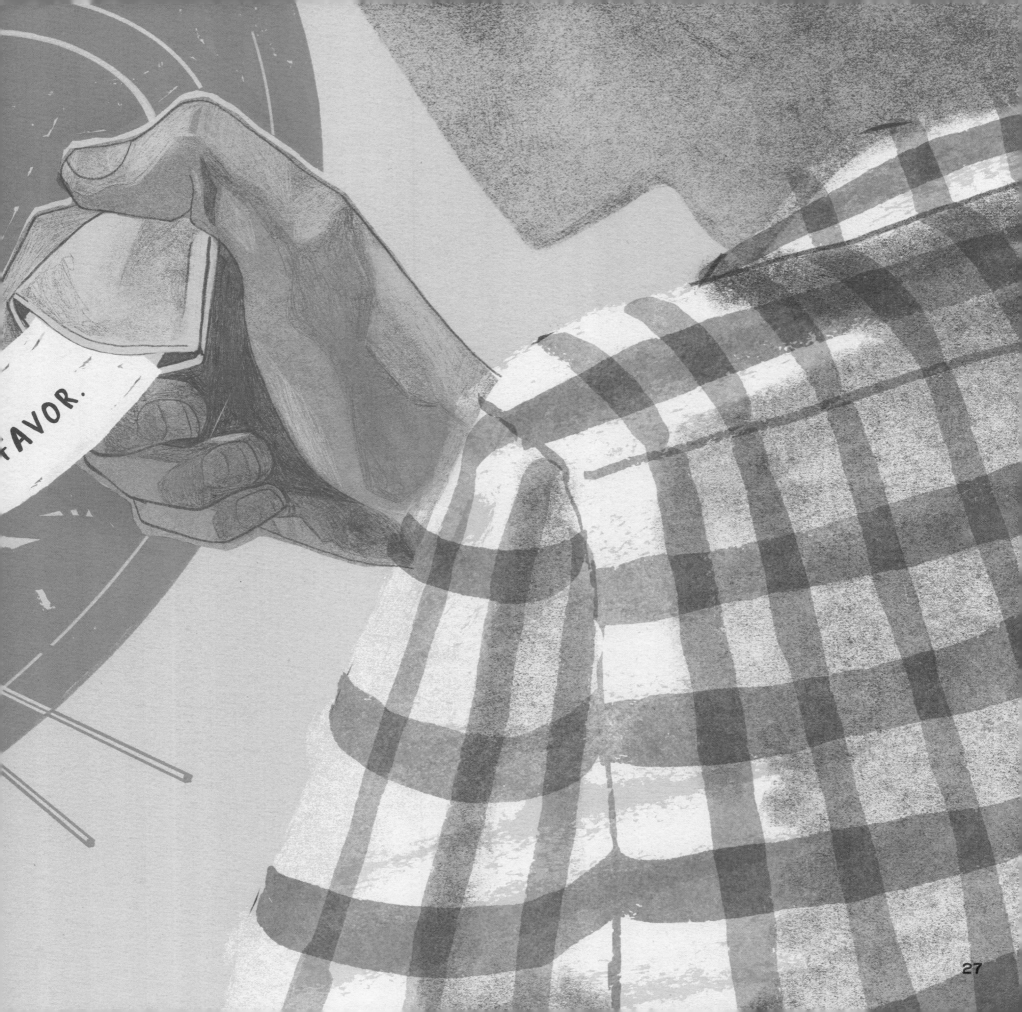

SIMON SAW A line snaking around the Supreme Court Building and down several blocks as he arrived. The Justices would now argue his case.

Would the court allow Asian Americans to reclaim a racist insult for their own— and allow The Slants to turn a negative into a point of pride?

♪"BUT NOTHING'S GONNA GET IN OUR WAY♪

AFTER AN HOUR-LONG hearing, it was all over. Simon took a deep breath—after eight years of fighting, it was now out of his hands. He walked out of the courthouse building, shocked to see more than one thousand people at the bottom of the steps.

"What are they doing here? Don't they know the court is in session? There are no public tours today."

Some had spent the frigid night in sleeping bags, hoping to get a seat to watch the case. When they saw Simon, they broke out into applause.

Would his battle be worth all the time and effort he'd put in?

♪**DON'T MAKE THE PEN
A WEAPON AND CENSOR
OUR INTELLIGENCE UNTIL
OUR THOUGHTS MEAN
NOTHING AT ALL**♪

ON JUNE 19, 2017, the Supreme Court ruled unanimously in
favor of The Slants!

"Dance rock band front man Simon Tam sought to trademark
The Slants. His aim was to reappropriate a term long used to
disparage a minority group and to render the term a badge of
pride. All of us agreed." —Ruth Bader Ginsburg

Simon had named his band to make a statement about racial
issues, but in the end, he fought to protect freedom of speech
for everyone.

Ruth Bader Ginsberg: A Supreme Court Justice for twenty-seven years until her death in 2020. She led the fight in the courts for gender equality.

Supreme Court Justices: The nine justices on the Supreme Court—one Chief Justice and eight Associate Justices—are the final authority to interpret the law and ensure that all Americans receive equal justice. At Simon's trial, only eight justices were present. Supreme Court Justice Antonin Scalia had just died. His replacement, Neil Gorsuch, had not yet started.

SING

♫ WE

"WHETHER IT IS on the stage or on the screen, we believe in the power of art to transform the world."

After the Supreme Court win, Simon and the members of the group started The Slants Foundation, a nonprofit organization dedicated to changing culture using arts and activism. His trademark battle song, "From the Heart," was featured in then President Barack Obama's "Act to Change" campaign as part of an anti-bullying message.

From punk musician to social activist, from inspirational speaker to book author, Simon continues to use the power of words—to change the world.

FROM THE HEART ♪

THE SLANTS®

In 2019, the band officially retired from touring to focus on their nonprofit organization, The Slants Foundation. The band continues to compose music but no longer performs. The Slants Foundation provides mentorship and scholarships for Asian American artists who want to incorporate activism into their work. Learn more at TheSlants.org. A portion of the proceeds of this book will be donated to The Slants Foundation.

OTHERS WHO HAVE FOUGHT ANTI-ASIAN RACISM

Simon Tam wasn't the first Asian American to fight against racism in our legal system. Asian Americans illuminated how racism existed in their court cases centered around the issues of immigration, citizenship, and workers' rights. Here are a few more . . .

CHY LUNG changed immigration policy. On March 20, 1876, the Supreme Court decided that Congress, not states, had the power to determine immigration laws.

YICK WO fought against discrimination. An ordinance in San Francisco required all laundries in wooden buildings to hold a permit but no permits were issued to Chinese owners. At the time, 89 percent of laundries were owned by workers of Chinese descent. On May 10, 1886, the Supreme Court determined that a race-neutral law administered in a prejudiced way violates the Fourteenth Amendment.

WONG KIM ARK fought for birthright citizenship. On March 28, 1898, the Supreme Court determined that all children born to alien parents on American soil qualify for U.S. citizenship.

TAKAO OZAWA fought for the right to become a citizen. On November 13, 1922, he was denied when the Supreme Court determined that "whiteness" was not determined by the color of one's skin but was specific to the Caucasian race.

BHAGAT SINGH THIND fought for the right to become a citizen. On February 19, 1923, he was denied when the Supreme Court ruled that individuals must have white skin and be of Caucasian descent to gain citizenship.

FRED KOREMATSU fought against the WWII internment of Japanese Americans. On December 18, 1944, the Supreme Court ruled against Korematsu.

KAJIRO OYAMA fought for land ownership for non-citizens. Starting in 1913 through the end of World War II, many states passed laws to prevent Japanese immigrants from purchasing or leasing property. On January 19, 1948, the Supreme Court struck down portions of California's notorious Alien Land Act.

KINNEY KINMON LAU fought for supplemental language instruction in the public schools. On January 21, 1974, the Supreme Court ruled that students who do not speak English must receive education to learn English.

AUTHOR'S SOURCES

Bernstein, Daniel. "Redskins name change timeline: How Daniel Snyder's 'NEVER' gave way to Washington Football Team." SportingNews.com. November 26, 2020.

Nuyen, Suzanne. "4 U.S. Supreme Court Cases Where Asian Americans Fought For Civil Rights." NPR. May 27, 2021.

Rose, Lisa. "5 Landmark Cases in U.S. History Spurred by Asian-Pacific Americans." NelsonMullins.com. May 29, 2020.

Tam, Simon. *Slanted: How an Asian American Troublemaker Took on the Supreme Court.* Nashville: Troublemaker Press, 2019.

Ziran, Dave. "Why the Cleveland Indians Will Change Their Name." The Nation.com. December 15, 2020.

The U.S. Supreme Court. Judicial Learning Center.com. Accessed 21, Sept 2021.

The Supreme Court receives about 10,000 petitions a year. If four of the nine justices decide that the case has merit, they will take the case. Generally, the Supreme Court hears 75–85 cases a year.

MIA WENJEN

I was one of the hundreds of Asian Americans who Simon Tam asked to write a letter of support for his case. I was struck by Simon's eloquence and determination to fight against an invisible form of racism—structural racism in our court system. I wrote my own letter of support as an Asian American blogger and watched on social media as his battle unfolded. When he wrote that his case would be decided by the Supreme Court, I was struck by the fact that there have only been a handful of Asian American cases heard by the Supreme Court.

SIMON TAM

While fighting our legal battle, I knew it was important to get as much attention and support from the Asian American community as possible. However, I also wanted to engage with so many folks so I could get a broader perspective on our work. How was it affecting others? How did they feel about the idea of reappropriation? What could we do to ensure that our work was equitable and just? Through those efforts, I met incredible folks like Mia, who represented the vast and diverse community that we served.

After I had some time to reflect on our journey, I wanted to capture the story in my own words because many of the media outlets that covered the issue failed to give it the kind of depth and nuance that I believed to be critical. Many wanted to compare our struggle for reclaiming identity with efforts in changing the racist Washington football team name; others only felt that it was a free speech issue that had nothing to do with race.

However, none of that was a complete picture of what it meant to overcome institutionalized discrimination in our government. I've always known that our stories matter—it was time for me to live up to that creed and put my own story to paper.

FROM THE HEART

*The Slants wrote this song as an anthem describing their trademark battle with the
US Patent & Trademark Office. Lyrics from this song are featured on each page.*

Sorry if our notes are too sharp
Sorry if our voice is too raw
Don't make the pen a weapon
And censor our intelligence
Until our thoughts mean nothing at all

Sorry if you take offense
You made up rules and played pretend
We know you fear change
It's something so strange
But nothing's gonna get in our way

There's no room
For your backward feelings
And your backyard dealings
We're never gonna settle
We're never gonna settle

No, we won't remain silent
Know it's our defining moment
We sing from the heart
We sing from the heart

No, we won't be complacent
Know it's a rock n roll nation
We sing from the heart
We sing from the heart

Sorry if we try too hard
To take some power back for ours
The language of oppression
Will lose to education
Until the words can't hurt us again

So sorry if you take offense
But silence will not make amends
The system's all wrong
And it won't be long
Before the kids are singing our song

There's no room
For your backward feelings
And your backyard dealings
We're never gonna settle
We're never gonna settle

No, we won't remain silent
Know it's our defining moment
We sing from the heart
We sing from the heart

No, we won't be complacent
Know it's a rock n roll nation
We sing from the heart
We sing from the heart

The Slants. *The Band Who Must Not Be Named,* 2017
Music & Lyrics: The Slants
Used by permission of The Slants LLC